WISDOM FROM

The Old Farmer's Almanac Book of Everyday Advice

Edited by Judson D. Hale, Sr.

PETER PAUPER PRESS, INC.
WHITE PLAINS, NEW YORK

The text in this book is excerpted from
The Old Farmer's Almanac Book of Everyday Advice edited by Judson Hale,
originally published in the U.S. by Random House, Inc.
Text copyright © 1995 by Yankee Publishing Inc.

Photo credits appear on page 77.

Designed by Heather Zschock

THE OLD FARMER'S ALMANAC® and DESIGN MARK®
are owned by, and used under authority of, Yankee Publishing Incorporated.

Published in 2005 by Peter Pauper Press, Inc.
in arrangement with Yankee Publishing Inc.

Peter Pauper Press, Inc.
202 Mamaroneck Avenue
White Plains, NY 10601
All rights reserved
ISBN 1-59359-901-3
Printed in China
7   6   5   4   3   2   1

Visit us at www.peterpauper.com

WISDOM FROM

The Old Farmer's Almanac
Book of Everyday Advice

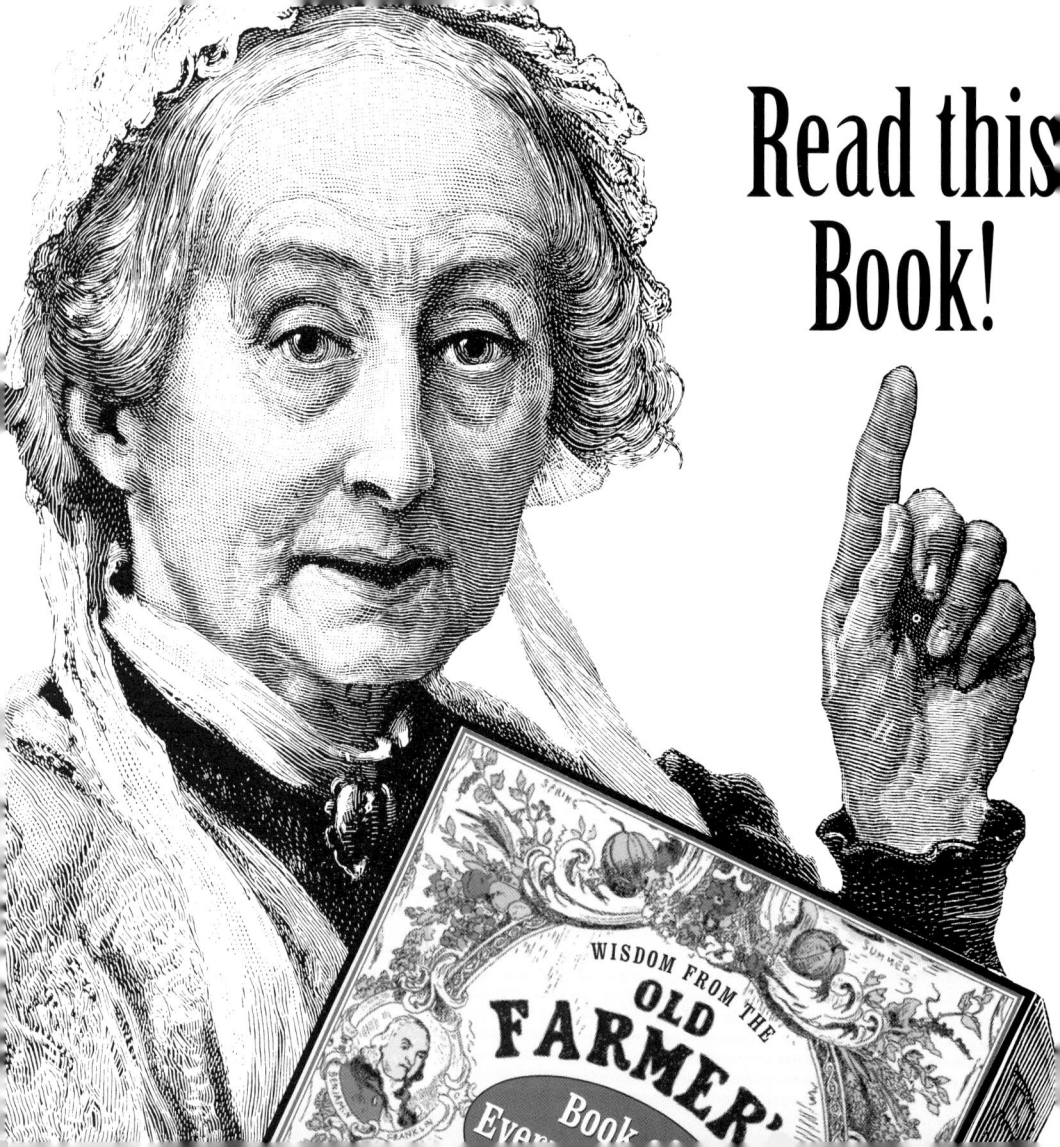

Read this Book!

WISDOM FROM THE
OLD FARMER'
Book
Ever

Contents

Introduction

I'*m pretty sure the best advice I've ever received (so far) was from my uncle, the late Robb Sagendorph, the eleventh editor of* The Old Farmer's Almanac. *No, it was not about "doing everything in moderation." That has become so tiresome. It wasn't that you should treat people as you'd want to be treated yourself either. No, it was far better than those old bromides.*

"Don't ever give advice," he said, solemnly. I nodded, waiting for more. I wasn't disappointed. "Unless," he said, after a long, thoughtful pause, "unless you can somehow determine what advice the person wants to hear. Then give that."

In the ensuing years, I've learned a lot about advice and

advice giving because that's what The Old Farmer's Almanac *does every year.*

I would have one piece of personal advice for anyone about to read this book: Please don't feel compelled to read it cover to cover, say, in one sitting. Instead, peruse it from time to time, choosing the sort of advice you're in the mood for on a particular day. After all, one can digest only so much advice at one time. Perhaps even in one life. ◉

PART ONE

Advice for Your Home

Solving the Mysteries of Love (& Sex)

BY CHRISTINE SCHULTZ

FOR STARTERS, you should know that if you're a romantic, you're not alone. Scholars have mistakenly believed for too long that courtly love is a luxury invented by the twelfth-century troubadours in Provence and handed down to us through Western culture. Recently, they've learned (or admitted) that romantic love is, in fact, universal. That means you could stumble into romance almost anywhere—in the Australian outback, in the Amazon jungle, or even in the hills of Idaho.

You may wonder, nevertheless, what exactly to look for in a mate. Try measuring forearms. One study showed that

> You might want to take notes while you're reading this chapter.

men and women with the same size forearms were more likely to stay together. But if you forget your tape measure, the poets say not to worry—you'll know it when you see it: "Through the eyes love attains the heart:/For the eyes are the scouts of the heart" (Guiraud de Borneil). Surprisingly, some scientists agree that you should go with your instincts, since love at first sight most likely evolved to spur the mating process. Scholars tell us that despite all the worldwide variations, the one physical characteristic that attracts men and women in every culture is a good complexion.

But it's not just how you look; it's how you smell. Foul odors do little to induce affection. Here's why: Located in our nasal cavities are five

At the time of the first kiss, or perhaps even before, neuron messengers from his brain have keyed in to the subtle scent being released from her apocrine glands.

A recent American study showed that women initiate two-thirds of all sexual liaisons. Their pickup line goes like this: "Hi."

(IT WORKS 100 PERCENT OF THE TIME.)

million olfactory neurons waiting like postal workers to sort through some ten thousand recognizable odors. They mail these perfumed messages directly to the brain's emotional headquarters (what scientists call the limbic system).

And it's not just how you smell; it's how you taste. Consider the Kiss. Rhett Butler and Scarlett O'Hara did it best in *Gone with the Wind* — Americans rate that the most memorable kiss in movie history. (Runner-up is the beach kiss by Burt Lancaster and Deborah Kerr in *From Here to Eternity*.) Don't think for a minute that a kiss is just a kiss. On the contrary, it speaks volumes. The esteemed Dr. Bubba Nicholson wrote in the *British Journal of Dermatology* that kissing allows us to taste semiochemicals on a suitor's skin. Semiochemicals, according to Nicholson, transmit biological signals of attraction and compatibility. In the words of Carl Jung, "The meeting of two personalities is like the contact of two chemical substances: if there is any reaction, both are transformed."

If you and your partner taste good to each other, you may well fall in love. You may find yourselves dizzy with excitement, full of bumbling energy that keeps you up late into the night.

Lovers should, in all cases, be advised to let the stomach settle before proceeding to the bedroom. "Sexual indulgence just after eating is nearly certain to be followed by indigestion, even if it does not cause immediate vomiting."

—CHRISTINE SCHULTZ

You might say that there's chemistry between you and your mate. And it would be true, literally. Michael Liebowitz of the New York State Psychiatric Institute says that during infatuation, the brain releases a chemical called phenylethylamine, or PEA, a natural amphetamine. When scientists inject PEA into mice, the animals jump and squeal, exhibiting "popcorn behavior."

Your best bet on the road to romantic love may be to stick to chocolates. Buried amid the calories are plenty of amphetamine-related substances sure to produce the erratic behavior common to infatuation. Food for the heart.

Almost anything you do concerning love would be better done under the waxing or full

Marriage is like eating an oyster. You can never tell whether it was bad or not until it's too late. -1943-

moon. Scientists and poets alike agree that the moon has a powerful effect on our reproductive beings. A statistically significant number of births (7 percent) occurs at full moons, and a study by Wesleyan University's psychology department found a 30 percent increase in sexual activity at the time of ovulation, which most frequently happens during the full moon.

But extended romantic bliss may become too much for the brains of the human. Liebowitz tells us that eighteen months is about all the brain can take in this revved-up state. Then the nerve endings become habituated to the stimulants, and PEA levels drop. A new set of brain chemicals called endorphins takes over. Endorphins calm the mind, kill pain, and reduce anxiety, leaving you and your partner comfortably settled in the attachment stage of love. Now you can talk, eat, and sleep in peace.

With all of these forces at play on our bodies, do our brains have any say at all in the matter of love?

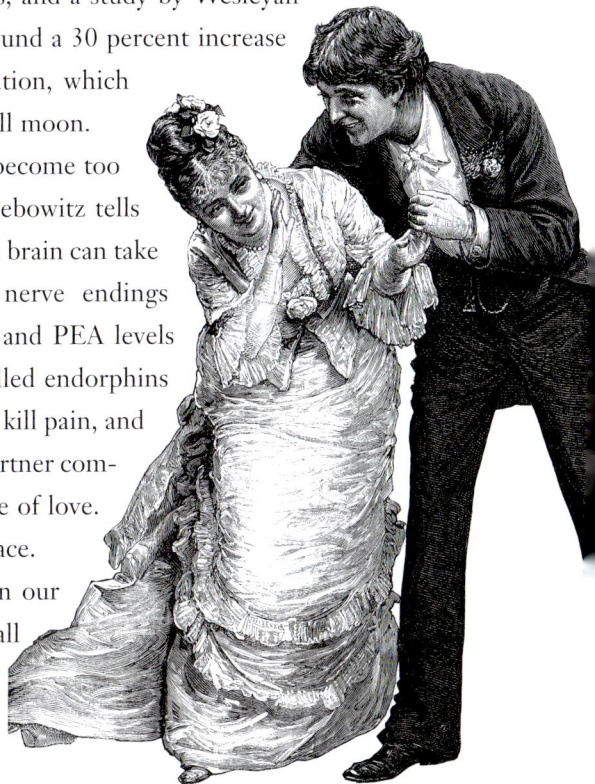

"Through the eyes love attains the heart: For the eyes are the scouts of the heart."

—GUIRAUD DE BORNEIL

How to Raise Perfect Children

*Although modern psychology frowns on thinking
of a child as a lump of bread dough, there are, in fact,
certain analogies between baking a fine loaf of
bread and raising a child to be proud of.*

BY SUSAN PEERY

*B*OTH BREAD BAKING AND CHILD REARING can be performed successfully without any prior experience. And although there are dozens of books of written recipes for both, the savvy baker and the wise parent soon realize that books can only give clues, for in real baking and real life, you have to do a lot of reading between the lines. Here's a baker's half dozen guidelines you can adapt to suit your circumstances.

1. SET ASIDE ENOUGH TIME. When baking bread, any attempt to hurry the rising and take shortcuts will result in an inferior product, crumbly and full of holes. Similarly, raising children takes time, and there's no way you can hurry through certain phases or skip any developmental stages, even if it's the stage where all the little

WISDOM FROM THE OLD FARMER'S ALMANAC BOOK OF EVERYDAY ADVICE

darling does is say "No!" and "Why?" Something complex and tasty is happening to the yeast (and the child) at every stage, something that will contribute to the ultimate flavor and texture.

2. USE FRESH INGREDIENTS FOR EVERY BATCH. Dedicated bakers often develop a sourdough starter that they use for successive bakings of bread, but the ingredients they add to the starter must be fresh, of the highest quality, and suitable for the desired result. Parents who decide to embark on more than one effort at child rearing might use the same "starter" to give a certain harmony to the family, but they will soon discover that the second child may have very different needs from the first, and ingredients will have to be varied accordingly.

3. PROVIDE A WARM ENVIRONMENT FOR THE DOUGH. Yeast breads are sensitive to temperature: too cold, and the yeast won't activate; too hot, and the yeast will die. The temperature range that's right has plenty of latitude — it's the extremes that cause failure. Children also need warmth, and plenty of it, lest they fail to thrive, but not so much that they smother. And without that basic, life-giving warmth, all the educational toys, great books, and natural-fiber baby clothes in the world won't make a whit of difference.

4. KNEAD WITH A LIGHT BUT FIRM TOUCH. The baker must knead thoroughly, turn the dough often, pat it gently, get to know its character, and handle it with attention and consistency. On a bread-baking day, the baker knows that there's a lot of time for other activities between risings, just as long as he or she keeps one eye on the dough. Children, too, will thrive with the right mixture of independence and hands-on attention.

5. PREPARE FOR THE UNEXPECTED. The only way to do this is to be flexible enough to abandon preconceived notions about results. Have all the ingredients on hand for poppy seed bread—except poppy seeds? Substitute: try sesame seeds or raisins. Always dreamed of coaching your son's Little League team—except he wants to spend the summer practicing his clarinet? Adapt: take him into the city to hear some good jazz. Maybe your daughter will like baseball.

6. DON'T GET IN OVER YOUR HEAD. Don't promise to bake twenty loaves in one weekend if you have a small oven. As a parent, don't get stuck making rules you can't enforce. For instance, you can't really make children go to sleep—it's good enough to tell them that they must go to bed (hey, you can make it fun—cuddle up and read a story or two); they don't have to go to sleep. (Reverse psychology is especially effective with five-year-old contrarians, who will fall asleep in thirty seconds—right after you tell them they can stay awake if they want to.)

7. PRESENTATION MATTERS. Every good cook knows that you can dress up the plainest meal to make it seem special. The child-rearing corollary is this: Always buy the right lunch box. Fussy eaters can be dazzled by the right container, by sandwiches cut into star shapes with cookie cutters. Little hurts can be fixed with Kermit the Frog bandages. Reluctant readers can be lured into literacy gradually with judiciously chosen comic books. It's just the art of friendly persuasion, of getting your bread and your kids raised. ◉

Predicting How Many Children You'll Have

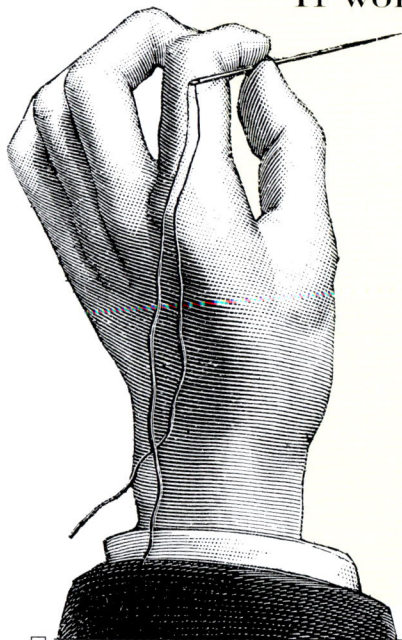

*F*irst, take an ordinary wooden pencil with an eraser and stick a threaded needle into the center of the eraser. Then lay your left arm on a table, with the palm of your hand facing up. Pick up the thread and dangle the pencil above your wrist. The pencil will begin to move. If it moves across your wrist, you'll have a boy. If it moves up and down your arm, you'll have a girl. The pencil will go in circles between each signal for more than one child, although twins *will be treated as one. It will come to a stop or wiggle when the count is finished. (Note: This works for men or women but not for women using birth control pills.)*

For those who doubt the veracity of this method, let me cite my own case. Several years ago, I had my tubes tied after I was divorced. At the time, I had two teenage sons, and the pencil would always stop after signaling two boys.

Then I married again and, for fun, tried the method on my new husband, who had no children. The pencil swung up and down his arm and then across his wrist—a girl and boy still to come! As for me, the pencil signaled two boys, a girl, and then another boy.

Well, I had my tubes untied and am now the mother of Eric, 18; Ben, 16; Collette, 3-1/2; and Jack, 20 months.

—COURTESY OF KAREN C. OKEY, ERIE, PENNSYLVANIA

Wise Words for the Good Cook

"You may make houses enchantingly beautiful, hang them with pictures, have them clean and airy and convenient; but if the stomach is fed with sour bread and burnt meats, it will raise such rebellions that the eyes will see no beauty anywhere." –1869–

NEVER EAT MORE THAN YOU CAN LIFT.

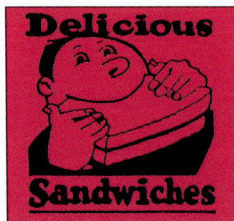

–MISS PIGGY–

Delicious Sandwiches

People eat finicky nowadays. When I was young, we relished blood sausage, brains and eggs, sheep-head soup, fish-head chowder, kidney stew, and mountain oysters —all good, solid, nourishing foods. Yet today's young-sters couldn't be paid to eat them.

MRS. A. KELLER, AGE 98
–1930–

The True Nature of Crumpets

They are shockingly plain, resemble pancakes, are rather chewy in texture, and, when made correctly, are frightfully good with a spot of tea, served with your best china — in the parlor.

By Judy Gorman

A long-time family friend recently remarked that as a child, I was inordinately preoccupied with food. Now that I think about it, I have to agree. For one thing, I was fascinated with the exotic foods described in storybooks. It was at fictional tea parties that I became acquainted with crumpets, which seemed a mysterious, yet elegant, accompaniment to tea. Of course, I had absolutely no idea what crumpets looked like, so I imagined them to be much like sugarplums, raspberry tarts, and other fanciful treats. Consider my surprise when, years later, I discovered their true nature.

Crumpets

½ cup warm water

1 package (1 scant tablespoon)
  dry yeast

1 teaspoon sugar

1 cup milk

2 tablespoons butter

½ teaspoon salt

2 cups all-purpose flour

½ teaspoon baking soda

1 tablespoon tepid water

In a large mixing bowl, combine the 1/2 cup warm water and the yeast. Add the sugar and stir to dissolve the yeast. Set aside.

In a small saucepan, heat 1/2 cup of the milk and the butter until the butter melts. Remove the pan from the heat and stir in the salt and the remaining 1/2 cup milk. Set aside to cool to room temperature.

When cooled, add the milk mixture to the yeast mixture and stir to blend. Mix in the flour with a wooden spoon. The batter will be very lumpy. Cover the bowl with plastic wrap, securing it with a rubber band. Set aside to rise for 1-1/2 hours, or until the bubbling action slows and the mixture begins to collapse in on itself.

Place four crumpet rings on a griddle, allowing the sides to touch.

Set over medium heat. Spray all the surfaces lightly with vegetable oil. Dissolve the soda in the 1 tablespoon tepid water and stir into the batter. The batter will be moist and ropy. When the griddle is hot, take up the batter by scant quarter cupfuls and pour it into the rings. Spread the batter to the sides with the back of a spoon.

As the batter begins to set, carefully rotate the rings to ensure even cooking. When the surface of the crumpets is covered with holes and no longer looks wet (about 3 minutes), remove the rings with tongs. Turn the crumpets over and continue cooking for about 1 minute more, or until the surface is lightly browned. Repeat with the remaining batter, spraying the rings and griddle before each batch. Cool the crumpets on a wire rack. Toast before serving.

Makes 10

PART TWO

Advice for Your Life

"Turn Over, Dear, for God's Sake, Turn Over!"

BY JIM COLLINS

Snoring levels up to 90 decibels—equivalent to a pneumatic jackhammer—have been recorded, and an estimated 50 million Americans snore.

WHO SNORES THE MOST?

As the old adage goes, "Laugh and the world laughs with you. Snore and you sleep alone." True, but if you do snore, you aren't alone in your isolation. An estimated fifty million Americans are afflicted with the ailment. And you certainly aren't in poor company. Twenty of the first thirty-two U.S. presidents were known to snore, including Washington, Lincoln, both

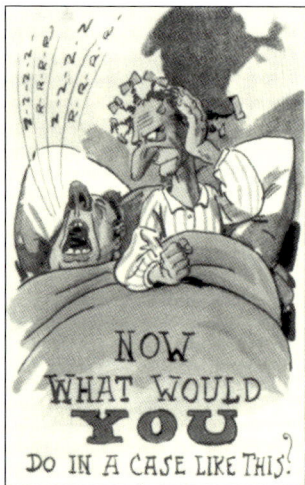

Adamses, both Roosevelts, Taft, Hoover, and Grant. So were Mussolini (he was renowned), Hemingway, Lord Chesterfield, and even Beau Brummell, the ladies' man.

How to Fall Asleep Quickly
– 1854 –

How to get to sleep is, to many persons, a matter of high importance. Nervous persons, who are troubled with wakefulness and excitability, usually have a strong tendency of blood to the brain, with cold extremities. The pressure of blood on the brain keeps it in a stimulated or wakeful state, and the pulsations in the head are often painful.

Let such rise and chafe the body and extremities with a harsh towel, or rub smartly with the hands, to promote circulation, and withdraw the excessive amount of blood from the brain, and they will fall asleep in a few moments. A cold bath, or sponge

bath, and rubbing, or a good run, or rapid walk in the open air, or going up and down stairs a few times, just before retiring, will aid in equalizing circulation and promoting sleep.

These rules are simple and easy of application in castle or cabin, and may minister to the comfort of thousands who would freely expend money for an anodyne to promote "Nature's sweet restorer—balmy sleep."

> The best way to go to sleep easily and quickly at night is to go to bed with a clear conscience.
>
> —BENJAMIN FRANKLIN

PLAIN HONEY LEFT ON YOUR LIPS OVERNIGHT WILL HAVE THE SAME EFFECT AS PETROLEUM JELLY— LEAVING THEM MOIST AND SHINY. ONLY HONEY DEFINITELY MAKES FOR TASTIER DREAMS.

MARGARET ROSS
–1977–

Taking a Bath Will Help You Live Longer

Just 2 to 5 quarts of nice, cold water every day . . .

*E*xtend the same favor, daily, to your whole person, that you do to your face and hands. All you require is two to five quarts of cold water (and as much more as you please) and one or two towels; the whole operation need not occupy five minutes. When you can faithfully and fearlessly wash yourself all over with cold water daily, you will have taken a vast step in the commencement of uninterrupted health. ◉

ADVICE ON SOCIAL SITUATIONS
Around the Dining Room Table

*M*OST DINING ROOM ADVICE in the old Almanacs had to do with manners, and each rule invariably contained the word "don't." Much of this chapter deals with an entirely different aspect of dining room behavior: the always-tricky art of conversation. Like when you've been seated between two strangers at a formal dinner party knowing that each one's good impression of you could benefit, say, your career. And yet you feel you have nothing to say. Perhaps a careful reading of the following pages will prove to be of some assistance.

Those awkward moments at a dinner party often require special skills.

How to Appear to Know More Than You Really Do

By Tim Clark

ANDOR IS A CRIPPLING DEFICIENCY IN POLITE SOCIAL INTER-COURSE. Don't misunderstand me—I'm not advocating lying. Lying is immoral. Lying is unethical. Lying can get you caught. And finally, lying is too easy. We are talking about a high art here, an art akin to bullfighting. Like the great matador, the *torero* of the dining room table is marked by his (or her) ability to dodge, to weave, to dance on the edge of disaster.

I once met a man whose impudence and skill at evading the onrushing horns of his interrogators made me want to shout, "Olé!"

If, for example, someone asked him, "Have you read *Don Quixote?*" he would say, "Not recently." Of

course, he'd never read it at all, but why disrupt a perfectly congenial conversation?

On another occasion, when asked if he had read Dante's *Inferno*, he replied, "Not in English." I was awestruck. In three absolutely truthful words, he managed to convey three distinct and misleading messages: (1) that he had read the book; (2) that he was fluent in Italian; and (3) that he was the sort of literary purist who would never settle for a mere translation. Glorious.

But you don't have to be Manolete to sling the bull. All you have to do is memorize a few Safe Subjects, All-Purpose Adjectives, Multifaceted Facts, and Irrefutable Opinions.

continued

✲ SAFE SUBJECTS ✲

A SAFE SUBJECT IS ONE that is interesting and provocative enough to allow you to make broad statements of dubious value, but at the same time is obscure or complicated enough that nobody but an expert will be able to call your bluff.

Here are a few Safe Subjects you might wish to consider:

1. QUANTUM PHYSICS: For ambiguity, it's hard to beat. It gave Einstein fits, and the best-known part of it is something called The Uncertainty Principle.

2. THE DEAD SEA SCROLLS: Discovered in 1947, these ancient texts have been studied ever since by a small group of biblical scholars who won't let anyone else take a look, probably because they still haven't figured out what they mean.

3. JAMES KNOX POLK: One of a series of one-term presidents preceding the Civil War, he was elected in 1844 and declined to run for a second term. Not very interesting in himself, he's a convenient guy to bring up if you get tired of somebody at the table who is

WISDOM FROM THE OLD FARMER'S ALMANAC BOOK OF EVERYDAY ADVICE

yammering on about the current occupant of the White House. Then *you* say, "What about James Knox Polk?"

The person talking is stopped cold. "What about him?" he says belligerently.

"Well, everything you just said could also apply to James Knox Polk," you reply. "And look what happened to him. He declined to run for a second term."

Everyone nods. Who could argue with that?

❧ ALL-PURPOSE ADJECTIVES ❧

THESE ARE DESCRIPTIVE TERMS THAT APPLY to almost anything. When asked to comment on a book, play, film, or musical composition of which you are completely ignorant, you should say:

"I prefer his (her) earlier works. They're more *pristine*." (Relatively few people know what "pristine" means. One of its meanings is "earlier.")

Or, alternatively:

"I prefer her (his) later works. They're more *mature*."

When a man says, "I lie," does he lie or does he speak the truth? If he lies, he speaks the truth; if he speaks the truth, he lies.

–1870–

continued

❧ MULTIFACETED FACTS ❧

YOU CAN SOUND LEARNED WITHOUT BEING VERBOSE. The strategic insertion of a single unusual piece of information can leave your fellow diners with a lasting impression of erudition.

For example, the author D.H. Lawrence's wife, Frieda, was the sister of Baron von Richthofen, the famous German flying ace. This is a valuable piece of trivia because it can be dropped casually into a discussion of any of the following subjects:

1. D.H. LAWRENCE

2. THE "RED BARON"

3. TWENTIETH-CENTURY ENGLISH LITERATURE

4. WORLD WAR I

5. IN-LAWS

6. SEX (ANY REFERENCE TO D.H. LAWRENCE IS APPROPRIATE IN THIS AREA)

7. SNOOPY

❧ IRREFUTABLE OPINIONS ❧

AT SOME POINT IN ANY DINNER CONVERSATION, someone is bound to turn to you and say, "What do you think?"

You don't want to say what you really think, because you haven't been paying attention. You have actually been thinking about the funny noise you heard in your car on the way over, or wondering why your hostess bought that hideous painting on the wall, or trying to remember the name of the actress who played Mary Ann on "Gilligan's Island." But you can't admit that. This is where you need to express an opinion that is relevant to any subject, and impervious to contradiction. Here are three good ones:

"It all depends."

"You can't generalize."

"Things are different in the South." ◉

CONVERSATION ENHANCER

How Happy Is a Clam?

By Tim Clark

We will probably never know exactly what makes a clam happy, but people usually list a long life and true love among their hopes. Thus, by human standards, a clam has good reason to be happy, because according to Ida Thompson of Princeton University, the clam is the foxy grandpa of the invertebrate kingdom. Thompson has determined that the bands one finds on a clamshell correspond to the rings found in a tree trunk and can be used to determine the clam's age. By this method, she has discovered that clams live as long as 150 years (assuming they are not made into chowder), show no signs of aging (other than adding bands), and remain sexually active throughout their lives. In fact, Thompson is uncertain whether clams ever die of old age.

Does Anyone Know the History of the Fork?

BY ALTHEA H. JACKSON

arly in the eleventh century, a woman journeyed from Byzantium to the Italian seaport of Venice. In 1070 she married a rich doge, Domenico Selvo. Now it so happens that the first person in written history to mention forks was the Italian St. Peter Damian, who was born in Ravenna in 1007 and died at Faenza in 1072. He wrote that the doge's wife from Byzantium "did not touch her food with her fingers, but carried it to her mouth with certain gold two-pronged forks" that she had brought with her from Byzantium. Everyone was shocked by the lady's extravagance, and few copied her example.

Never
put off to
yesterday
what you
can do
tomorrow!

–DWIGHT E.
GRAY

RULES TO LIVE BY

10 Rules of Behavior

(ACCORDING TO THOMAS JEFFERSON)

1. Never put off till tomorrow what you can do today.
2. Never trouble another for what you can do yourself.
3. Never spend your money before you have it.
4. Never buy what you do not want because it is cheap; it will be dear to you.
5. Pride costs us more than hunger, thirst, and cold.
6. We never repent of having eaten too little.
7. Nothing is troublesome that we do willingly.
8. How much pain have cost us the evils which have never happened.
9. Take things always by the smooth handle.
10. When angry, count ten before you speak; if very angry, a hundred.

Jefferson had a rule for every occasion.

IF 3 RULES ARE ENOUGH

*Keep your feet warm, your back straight,
and your head cool.* –1800–

If wisdom's ways you wisely seek, five things observe with care: of whom you speak, to whom you speak, and how and when and where.

—1851—

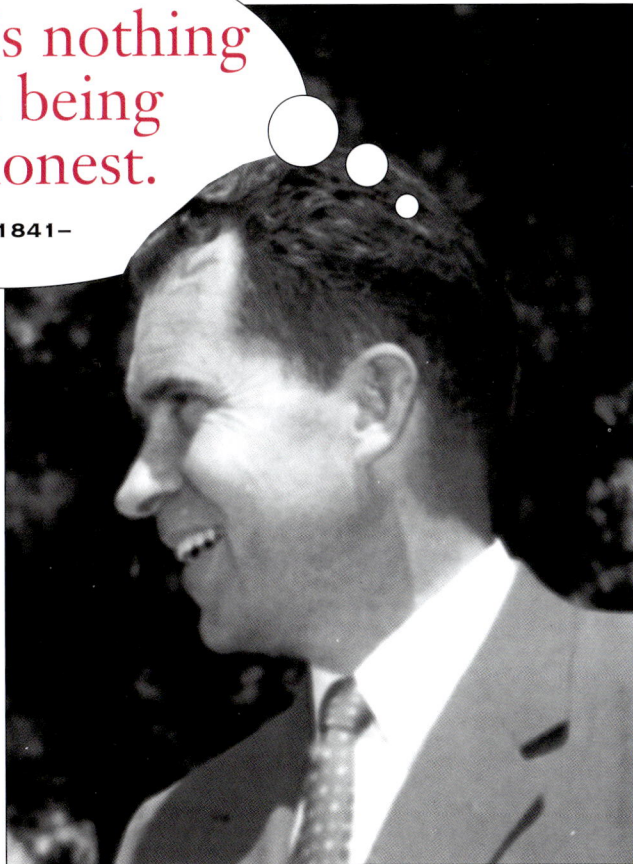

There is nothing
worth being
dishonest.

–1841–

EXPERIENCE
IS WHAT
ENABLES YOU
TO RECOGNIZE
A MISTAKE
WHEN YOU
MAKE IT
AGAIN.

–1947–

What to Say When You're Selling Your House

(And What It Means)

BY DAVID ARCHIE

"DOLLHOUSE" — Really cramped.

"COMFORTABLE" — Needs repairs.

"RUSTIC" — Badly needs repairs.

"RURAL SETTING" — The road is bad.

"IDEAL FOR ENTERTAINING" — You can't afford it.

"DECORATOR'S CHOICE" — Your wife will hate the colors.

"ALL-ELECTRIC KITCHEN" — Has garbage disposal.

"IMMEDIATE OCCUPANCY" — We've had a hard time moving this dog.

"SECLUDED LOT" — Bushes are way overgrown.

Rustic Charmer IN RURAL SETTING FOR IMMEDIATE OCCUPANCY.

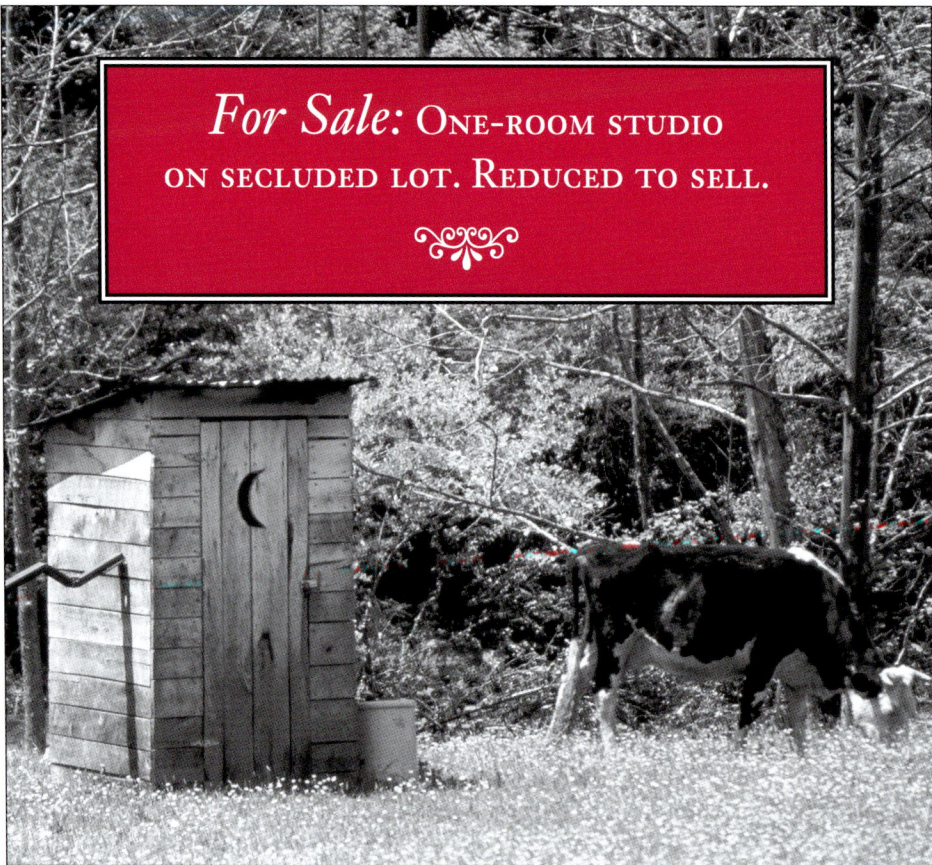

For Sale: One-room studio on secluded lot. Reduced to sell.

"Low taxes" — Neighborhood nearly ready for urban renewal.

"3–4 bedrooms" — If you can find a place to eat in the kitchen.

"Unbelievable" — Unbelievable.

"Panoramic view" — Just try to get up the drive in winter.

"Centrally located" — You'll have fun keeping watch on the bar next door.

"Modern" — Has indoor bathroom.

"Charming" — Ideal for a midget family.

"Chateau-like" — Mansard roof leaks.

"Executive" — Price is outrageous.

"Reduced to sell" — Price is still outrageous.

"Baronial living room" — Fireplace is too big to draw properly.

"Gleaming" — We really had to work to get this ready for sale.

"Victorian elegance" — The heating bills are interesting.

Don't Bother Reading Any Instructions But These

*G*rasp the gizmo in your left hand. With your right hand, insert the doohickey into the little whosit just below the bright red thingamajig and gently—gently!—turn it in a clockwise direction until you hear a click. Attach the long thingamabob to the whatchamacallit. Do not under any circumstances allow

the metal whatsit on the end to come in contact with the black plastic thingummy. Failure to follow these instructions will result in damage to the doodad.

Omigosh! or
Always Read the Fine Print

A Chicago woman attending the movies one day had a very bad headache and, groping in her purse, over a period of two hours took what she assumed to be five aspirin tablets, with no relief. When she left the theater, she discovered to her horror that she had taken concentrated food tablets for plants. Reading the label in fear and trembling to see if she had been poisoned, she found it all reassuring until she came to a footnote that read, "Each tablet is equivalent to one shovelful of manure."

—COURTESY OF GRACE SMITH BEERS

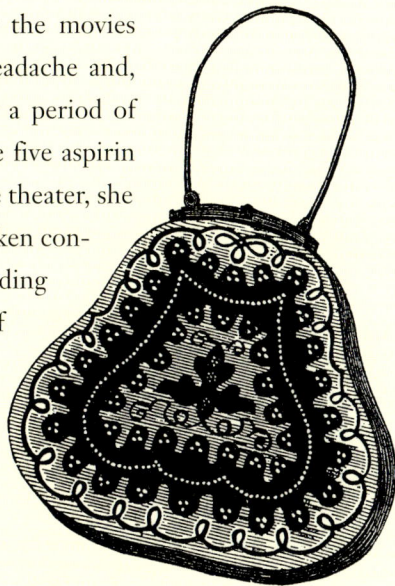

39 Ways to Avoid Dying

*All without giving up any of the stuff
you really like to do . . . or eat.*

BY TIM CLARK

*D*octors and scientists are always telling us how to live longer. Usually their suggestions involve a healthier diet or lifestyle: eating less fat and more vegetables and fruits, getting more exercise, or giving up smoking. We wholeheartedly endorse these rigorous and unpleasant methods of extending life. But our research into centuries of American folk wisdom has turned up thirty-nine easy ways of avoiding death by observing a few simple rules in everyday situations. These beliefs come from all over the country and were actually collected by students of folklore and anthropology. None of them was made up. Just remember: if you fail to observe these rules, we won't be responsible for the consequences.

❧ HOUSEKEEPING HINTS ❧

1. Don't take ashes out of the fireplace or stove between Christmas and New Year's Day.
2. Never place a broom on a bed.
3. Close umbrellas before bringing them into a house.
4. Avoid sweeping after sundown.
5. Never wash clothes on New Year's Day.
6. Don't, under any circumstances, shake out a tablecloth after dark.
7. Never wash a flag.
8. Keep cats off the piano keys.
9. Don't turn a chair on one leg.
10. Don't hang a dishcloth on a doorknob.
11. Never sweep under a sick person's bed; it will kill him or her.
12. Don't ever, ever rock an empty rocking chair.

continued

❧ RENOVATION & DECORATING ❧

13. Never add on to the back of your house.

14. Never drive a nail after sunset.

15. Don't move into an unfinished house.

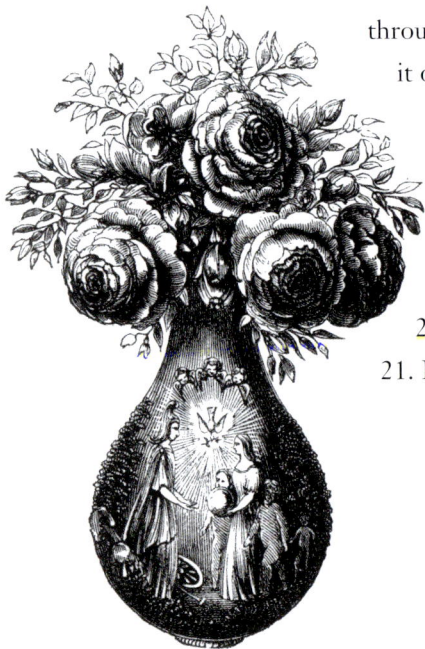

16. Avoid carrying axes, shovels, and other sharp-edged tools through a house. If you must take one inside, always take it out by the same door.

17. If you move out of a house, don't move back into it for a year.

18. Don't hang your sweetheart's picture upside down.

19. If a picture falls from the wall, don't pick it up.

20. Never carry a peacock's feather into a house.

21. Keep cut flowers out of bedrooms overnight.

❧ FASHION & SEWING ❧

22. Don't make new clothes between Christmas and New Year's Day.
23. Don't walk around in one shoe.
24. Never wear another's new clothes before he or she has worn them.
25. If you're a woman, don't make your own wedding dress. If you do, you will not live to wear it.

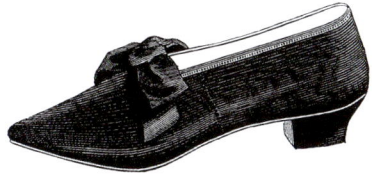

❧ COOKING & TABLE MANNERS ❧

26. Never set three lamps on a table at the same time.
27. Never serve thirteen at table.
28. Avoid drinking coffee at five o'clock.
29. Never return borrowed salt.
30. Don't ever cross knives while setting the table.
31. Be sure that someone else cooks your birthday dinner.
32. Don't put two forks at one place setting.
33. Never, never turn a loaf of bread upside down.

continued

❧ SLEEPING ❧

34. Never sleep with your head at the foot of the bed; this is surely fatal.
35. Don't sing in bed.
36. A man should never dream of a naked woman; a woman should never dream of a naked man. (You know who you are . . .)

❧ MISCELLANEOUS ❧

37. Try not to imagine it's Saturday when it's not.
38. Never sell a dog.
39. Don't even think about mocking an owl. ◉

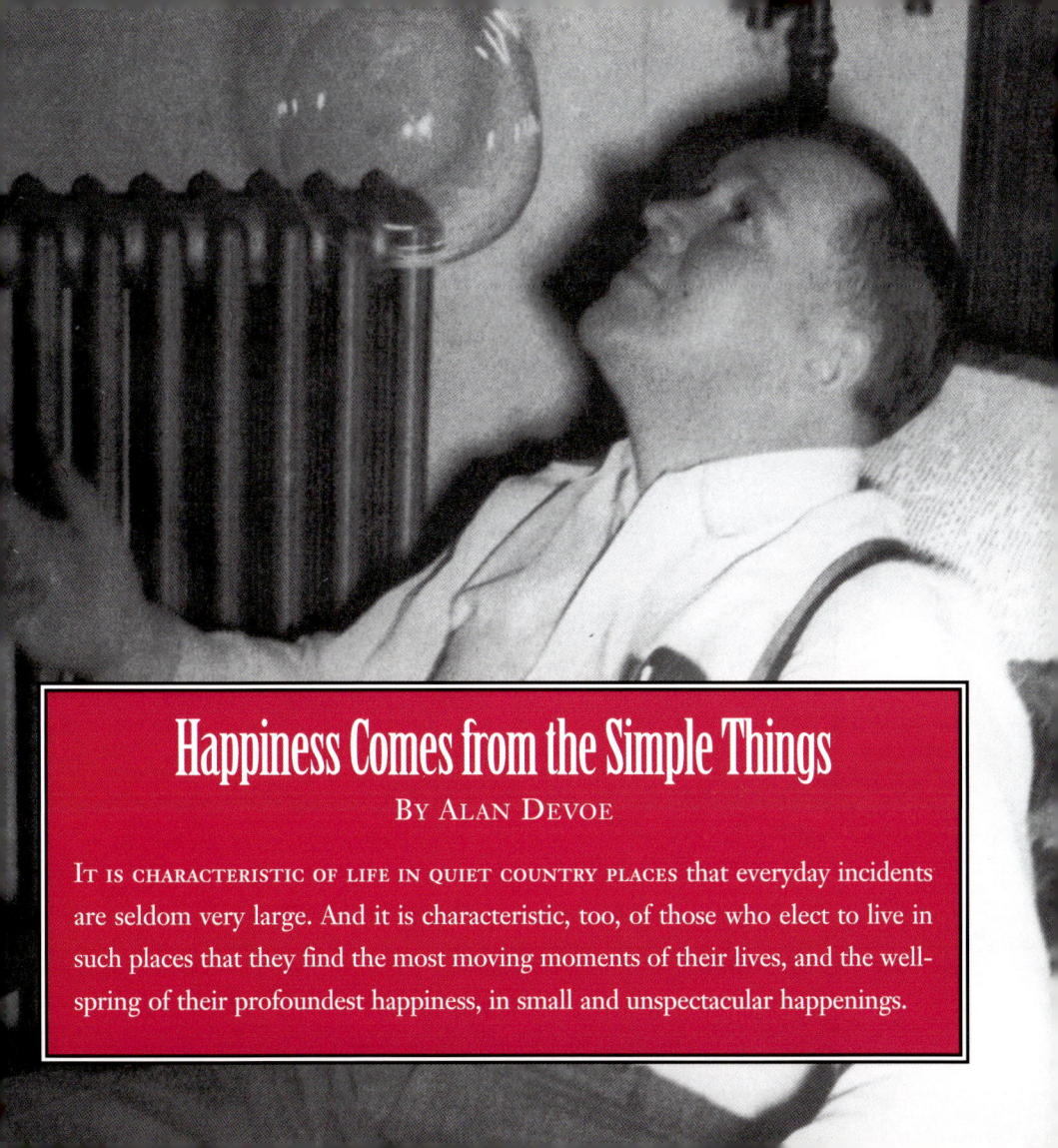

Happiness Comes from the Simple Things

By Alan Devoe

IT IS CHARACTERISTIC OF LIFE IN QUIET COUNTRY PLACES that everyday incidents are seldom very large. And it is characteristic, too, of those who elect to live in such places that they find the most moving moments of their lives, and the wellspring of their profoundest happiness, in small and unspectacular happenings.

How to Become Immortal

*Undying fame—or disgrace—can be had by
a person whose name becomes an eponym,
a part of the language. For example . . .*

BY TIM CLARK

❧ CONDOMS ❧

Legend has it that someone in the court of the rakish Charles II of England—a man named Condom—devised the prophylactic from animal intestines. Giovanni Casanova (1725–1798), an eponym himself, is said to have been a customer.

❧ JOSH ❧

Josh Billings, the pen name of Henry Wheeler Shaw (1818–1885), was a New England humorist, and some authorities believe that the word *joshing* can be traced to his popular jokes and stories. Others disagree, bringing to mind one of Billings's favorite sayings: "It is better to know nothing than to know what ain't so."

✌ LEOTARD ✌

Jules Leotard (1830–1870) was a French aerialist who not only invented the one-piece gymnastic costume but also was the first man to perform a somersault on the flying trapeze.

✌ NOBEL PRIZE ✌

The invention of dynamite and other explosives by Alfred Nobel (1833–1896) made him a fortune that he left in trust to establish prizes for peace, physics, chemistry, physiology and medicine, and literature. He saw no contradiction to this. "The day when two army corps will be able to destroy each other in one second," he wrote, "all civilized nations will recoil from war in horror and disband their armies."

continued

✂ SIDEBURNS ✂

Ambrose Burnside (1824–1881) went bankrupt making rifles in 1857, ordered the Union Army of the Potomac into an appalling slaughter at Fredericksburg in 1862, illegally jailed opponents of the war in Ohio, and finally left military life in disgrace after another debacle in 1864. Nevertheless, Rhode Islanders elected him to three terms as governor and then to the U.S. Senate, where he died in office. He is remembered chiefly for his long side-whiskers, called "burnsides" in his day, but later transmuted to "sideburns."

Remember the Human Coping Mechanism

Commenting on all the current prophesies of doom (and all prophecies down through the centuries have usually been of the doom variety), historian Barbara Tuchman said, "You cannot extrapolate any series in which the human element intrudes; that is, the human narrative never follows and will always fool the scientific curve . . . the doom factor sooner or later generates a coping mechanism."

Always leave home with a tender good-bye and loving words. They may be the last.

–1887–

> It is much better to know about the smallest vine twisting up the most remote canyon in the Rockies than to know the entire Grand Canyon in a glance.
>
> **—JOAQUIN MILLER**

Don't Underestimate What Your Friends Might Do

*D*uring the winter of 1976, Tennessee state senator Fred Berry was close to being the senate's official fossil for a few minutes. Berry, sixty-three, offered a bill to name an official state fossil, an official mineral, an official stone, and an official gem. Since the bill was offered late in the legislative session, it was amended by voice vote to make Berry the state's official fossil. Berry withdrew the bill.

Because of a miscalculation on his part, state senator Fred Berry of Tennessee came very close to becoming the official state fossil.

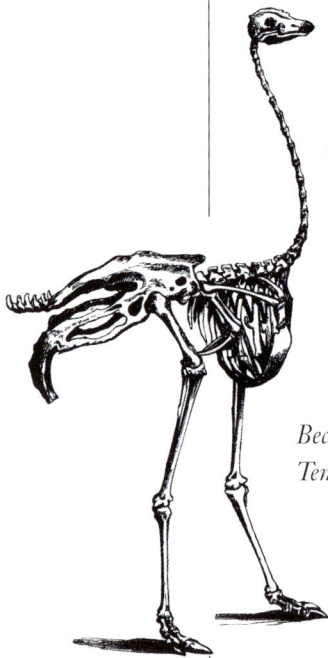

Famous Last Words
(ALL TRUE)

The common thread is a lack of sorrow, an absence of horror. In fact, last words are often something pleasant to recall during the subsequent gathering of family and friends in the parlor . . .

COLLECTED BY BOB QUARTERONI

*A*lthough it may seem morbid to some people, the collecting of last words is actually a very soothing occupation. As author Barnaby Conrad said, "After reading thousands of deathbed utterances, one is struck and comforted by how comparatively pleasant dying is reported to be. Especially when compared with other ordeals. Such as living, for example."

continued

For each weighty last phrase, there are dozens of mundane or humorous statements that I find edifying. It's nice to know that scholars and famous writers are human, too.

FOR EXAMPLE:

- Maria Mitchell, the first woman astronomer in America and a Nantucket native: "Well, if this is dying, there is nothing unpleasant about it."

- Clifton Fadiman once recalled a letter from a friend who wrote that when his father was dying, the nurse put her ear down close to the patient's face to see whether she could detect any breathing. The old gentleman opened his eyes and said, "Boo!"

- Henry David Thoreau, when he lay dying in 1862, was asked by a bedside companion if he had made his peace with God. Thoreau replied calmly that he was not aware of ever having quarreled with God. Then he uttered two enigmatic last words: "Moose . . . Indian . . ."

- When Ethan Allen, leader of the Green Mountain Boys, was

dying, a parson told Allen that a band of angels was waiting. Allen answered, "Waiting are they? Waiting are they? Well, Goddam 'em, let 'em wait!"

❀ James Rodgers, executed in 1960, was asked if he had any last request as he stood before a firing squad. "Why, yes," he said. "I'd like a bulletproof vest."

❀ William Palmer's last words, as he stepped on a gallows trap in 1856, were: "Are you sure it's safe?"

❀ When Henry Ward Beecher, the orator and preacher, was dying at age seventy-four, his doctor asked him how high he could raise his arm. He replied, "Well, high enough to hit you, Doctor."

❀ Richard Monckton Milnes, a Victorian politician, uttered this deathbed quip: "My exit is the result of too many entrées."

❀ Dominique Bouhours, a philosopher and grammarian, was concerned with sentence structure as he faced death: "I am about to

— or I am going to — die: either expression is used."

✳ Oscar Wilde called for champagne, saying, "I am dying, as I have
  lived, beyond my means."

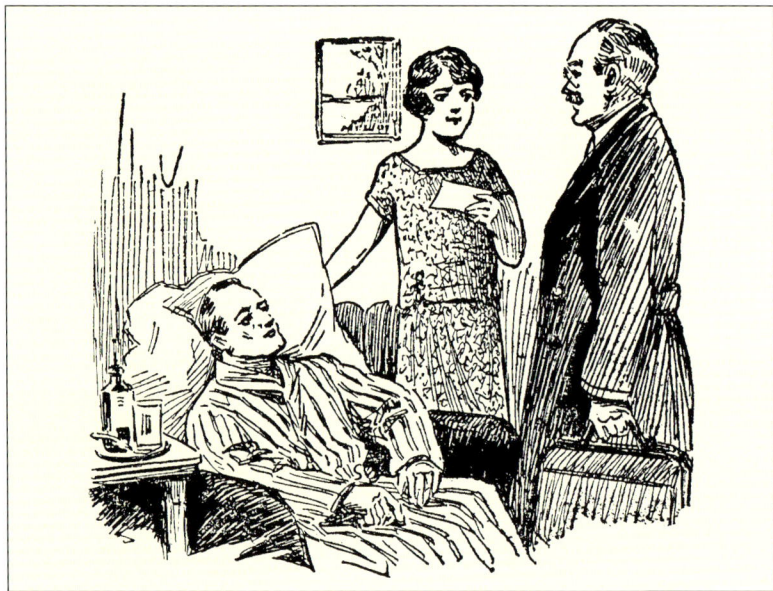

Wisdom from The Old Farmer's Almanac Book of Everyday Advice

Photo Credits